MILK

THROUGH THE EYES OF A CHEMICAL ENGINEER

DIANA TRAN

To My Dear Brother,
I am getting there with my books.

Remember this from...

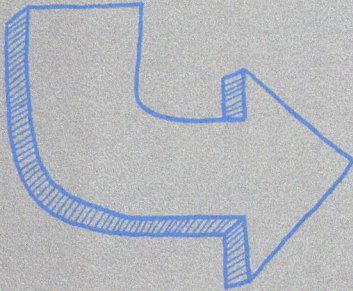

How does milk change into a powder?

The liquid milk is passed through a nozzle attached to a glass chamber where it changes into tiny droplets. The hot air helps to carry the droplets through as it dries into a powder. However, if the temperature is not correct the droplets will end up somewhere else!

To do this, a *spray drying* process is used.

Spray dryer image adapted from BUCHI Spray Dryer & Encapsulation Solutions, Particle formation for lab scale Brochure, www.buchi.com/spray-drying/solutions.

9

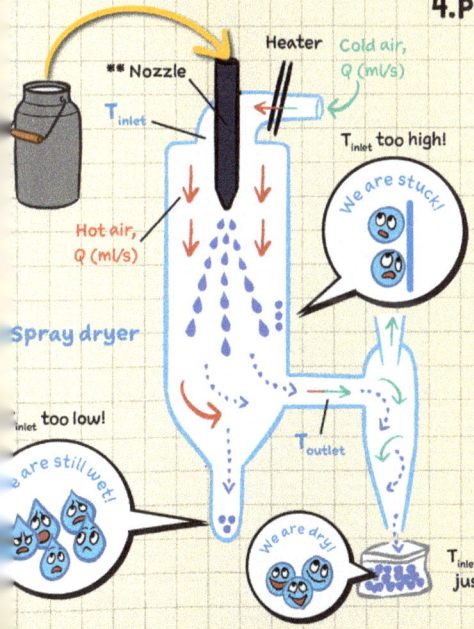

Rewind...

What if we don't want milk **powder**? How will we eat our favourite cereal, drink our coffee, or make fluffy scrambled eggs for breakfast in the morning?

4

In that case, we need to look at the unit operations within the **PROCESS** stage before the **PRODUCT** is created.

A **unit operation** is a unique chemical engineering term related to the types of equipment and processes used in scaling up laboratory chemistry.

It can involve transferring **heat**, **mass**, and **fluids**.

Try visualising smaller units arranged in an orderly row within a larger process.

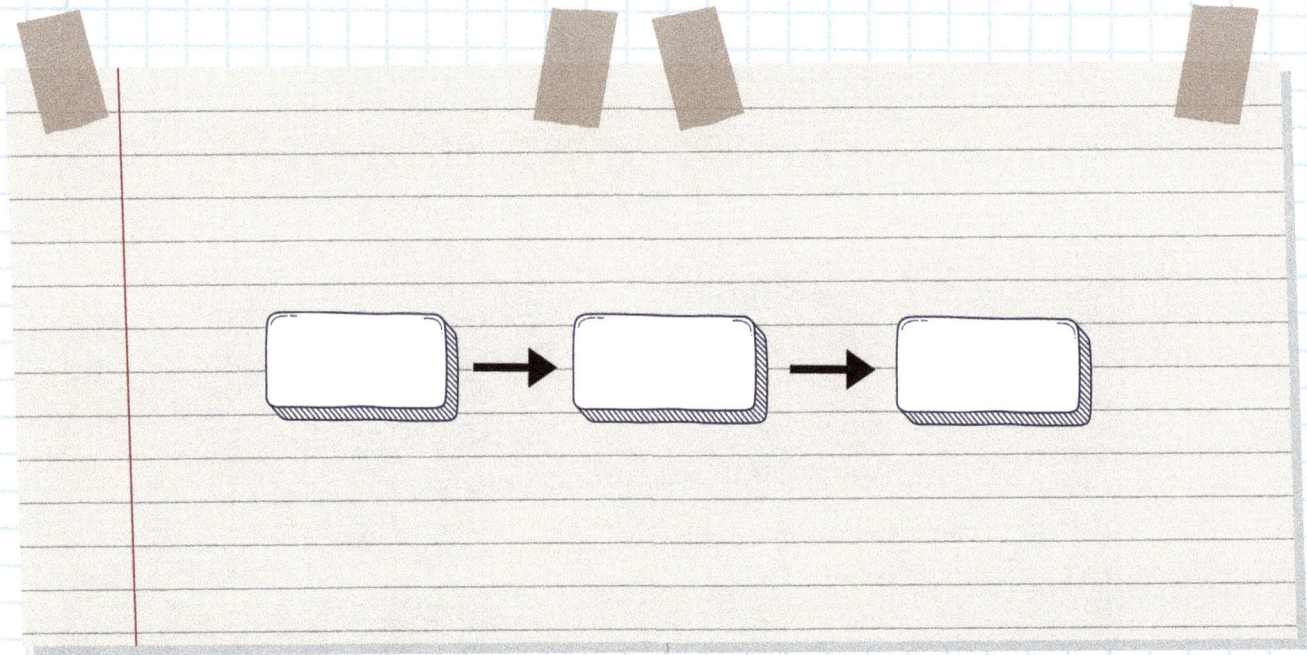

This can be shown as a **B**lock **F**low **D**iagram **(BFD)**.

Chemical engineers use BFDs to understand what is happening throughout the production process. Each block contains an operation.

Let's take a brief look at each one!

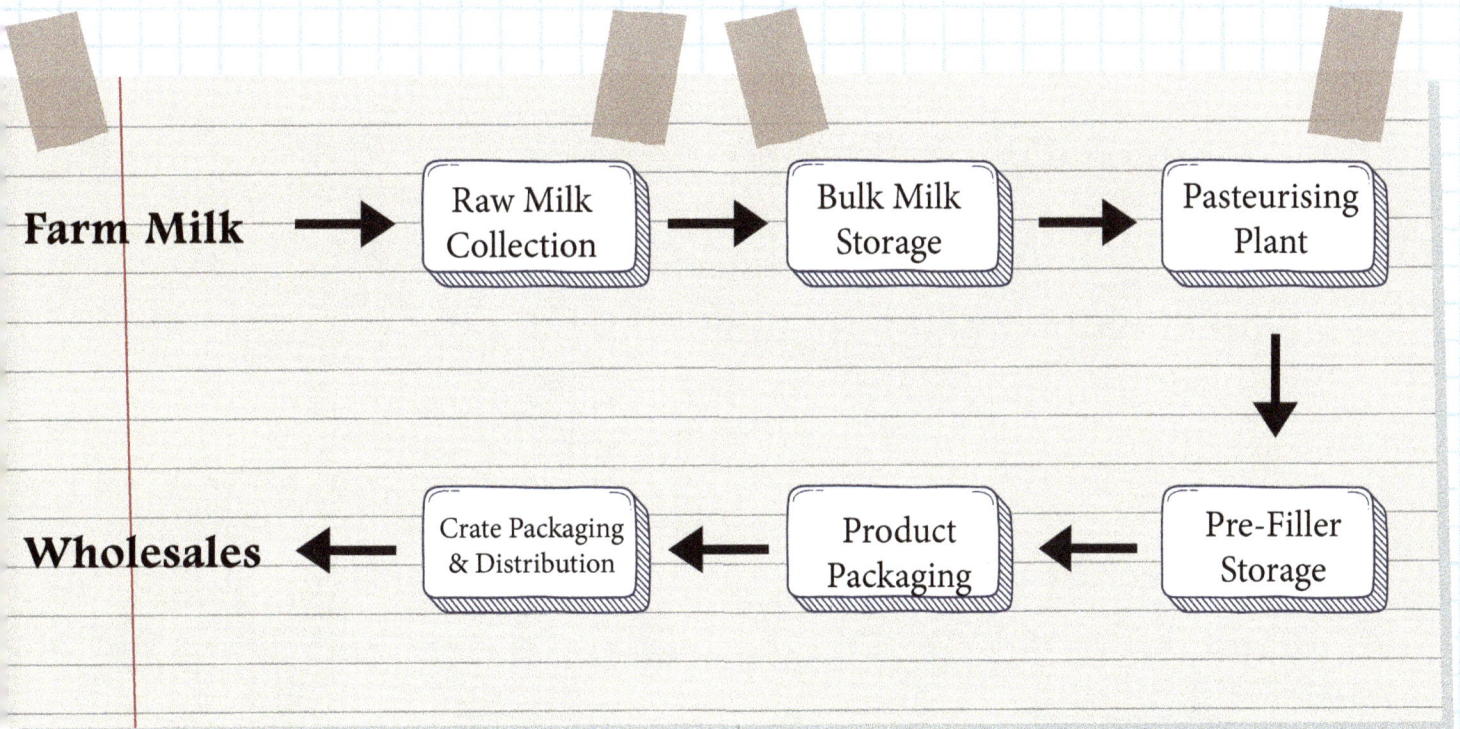

Farm Milk → Raw Milk Collection → Bulk Milk Storage → Pasteurising Plant ↓ Pre-Filler Storage ← Product Packaging ← Crate Packaging & Distribution ← **Wholesales**

Notes. 1. Operating conditions are not included. 2. Diagram is not drawn to scale.

Raw Milk Collection

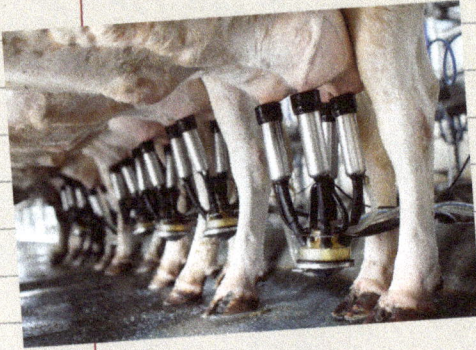

Once the raw milk is collected from dairy cows, the milk is stored in vats that are refrigerated below 4°C.

A sample of raw milk is tested to meet strict quality and composition specifications.

Quality
- ☑ Colour
- ☑ Odour
- ☑ Bacterial count
- ☐ Acidity
- ☐ Foreign contamination
- ☐ Free of residues

Composition
- ☐ Water
- ☐ Fat
- ☐ Protein
- ☐ Minerals
- ☐ Lactose

Bulk Milk Storage

The raw milk is delivered to a factory where it is pumped through a plate heat exchanger to achieve a temperature of 2°C before being transferred into storage silos.

An example of a simple plate heat exchanger.

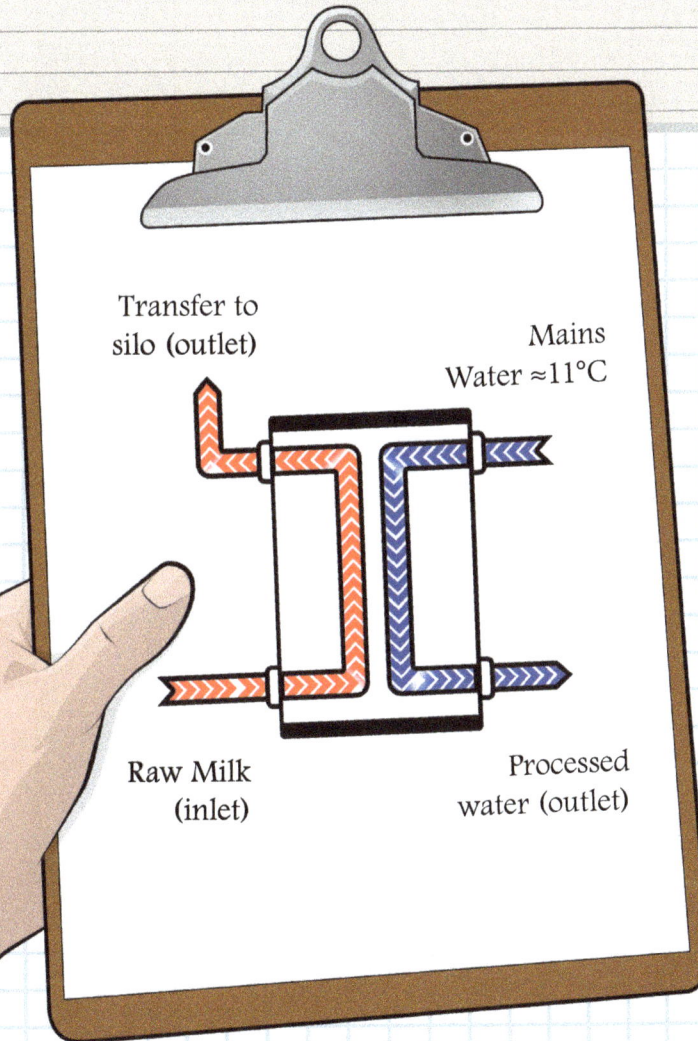

Transfer to
silo (outlet)

Mains
Water ≈11°C

Raw Milk
(inlet)

Processed
water (outlet)

Pasteurising Plant

From the silos, the raw milk is separated, homogenised, and pasteurised in the processing plant.

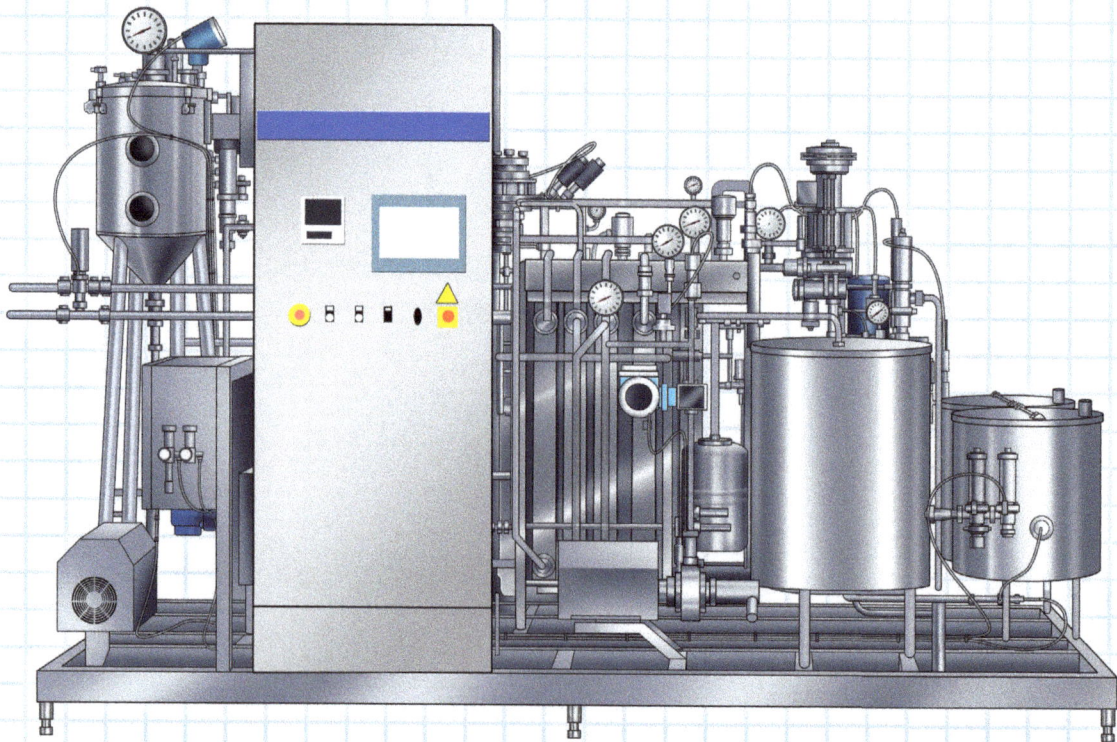

Pasteurisation at 74°C destroys harmful microorganisms that may be present in the raw milk.

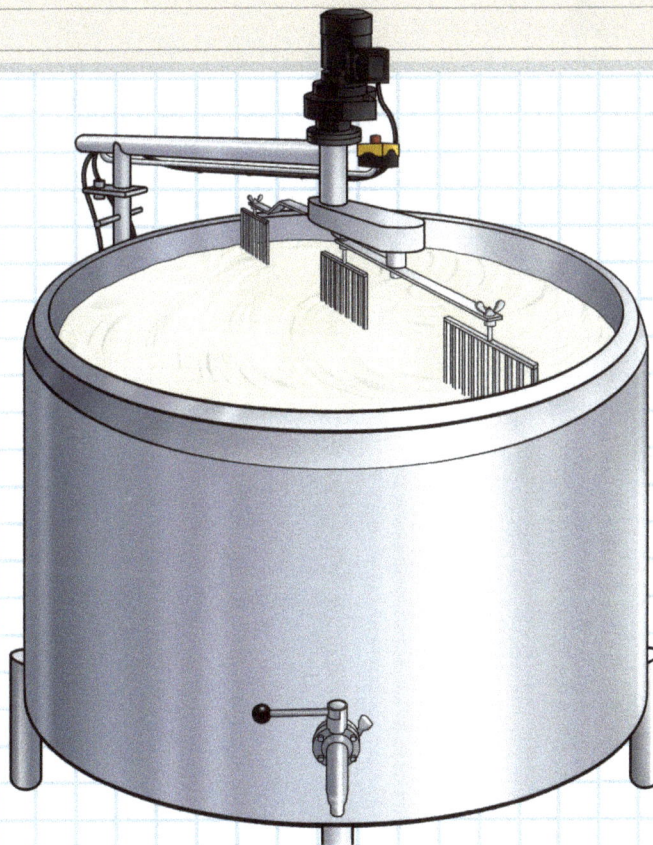

Hot

74°C

Homogenisation is used to ensure the cream is evenly dispersed in the milk with other ingredients (e.g. flavours, sugars) depending on the desired product. The fat/protein or fat/solids ratio in the milk can be different.

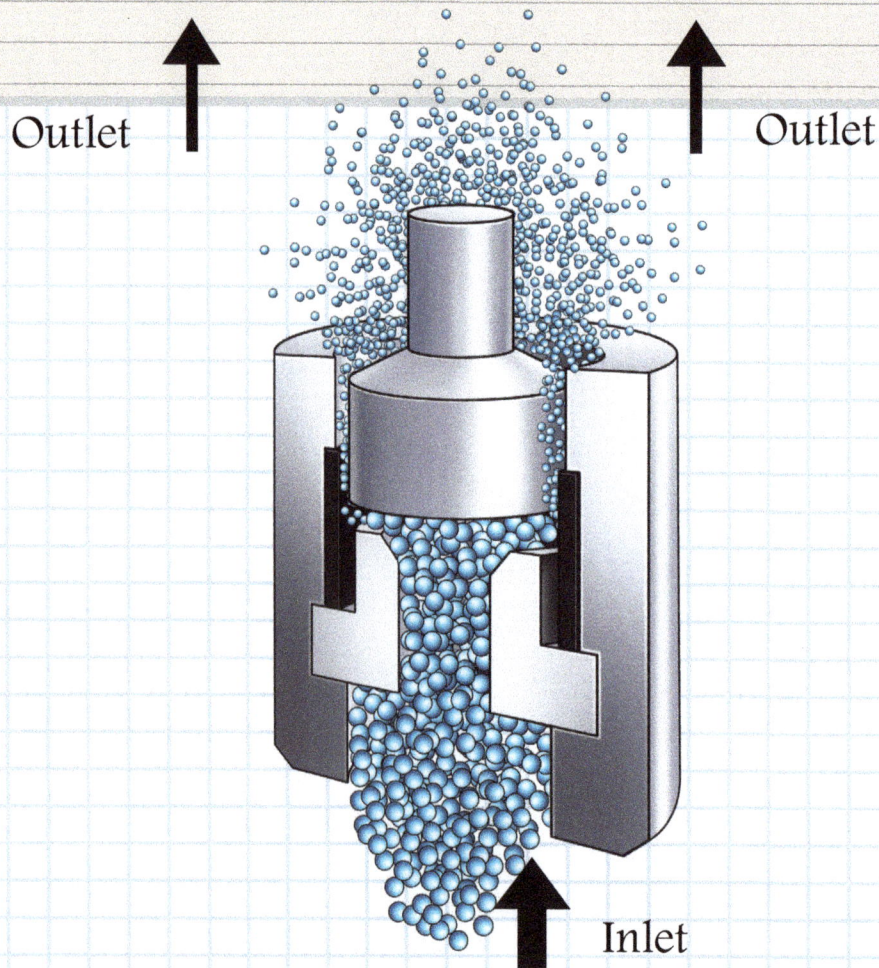

Outlet

Outlet

Inlet

Pre~Filler Storage

Each milk batch is then transferred to a sterilised tank that is stored at a temperature below 4°C.

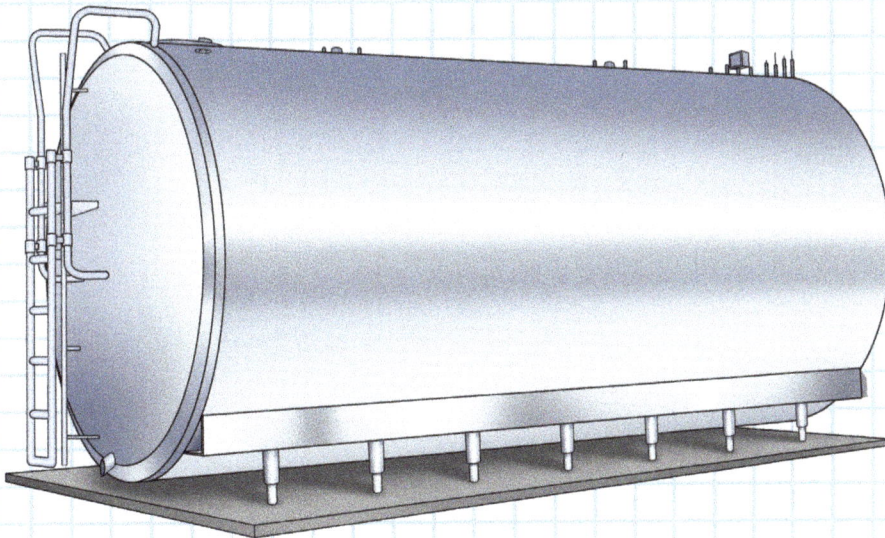

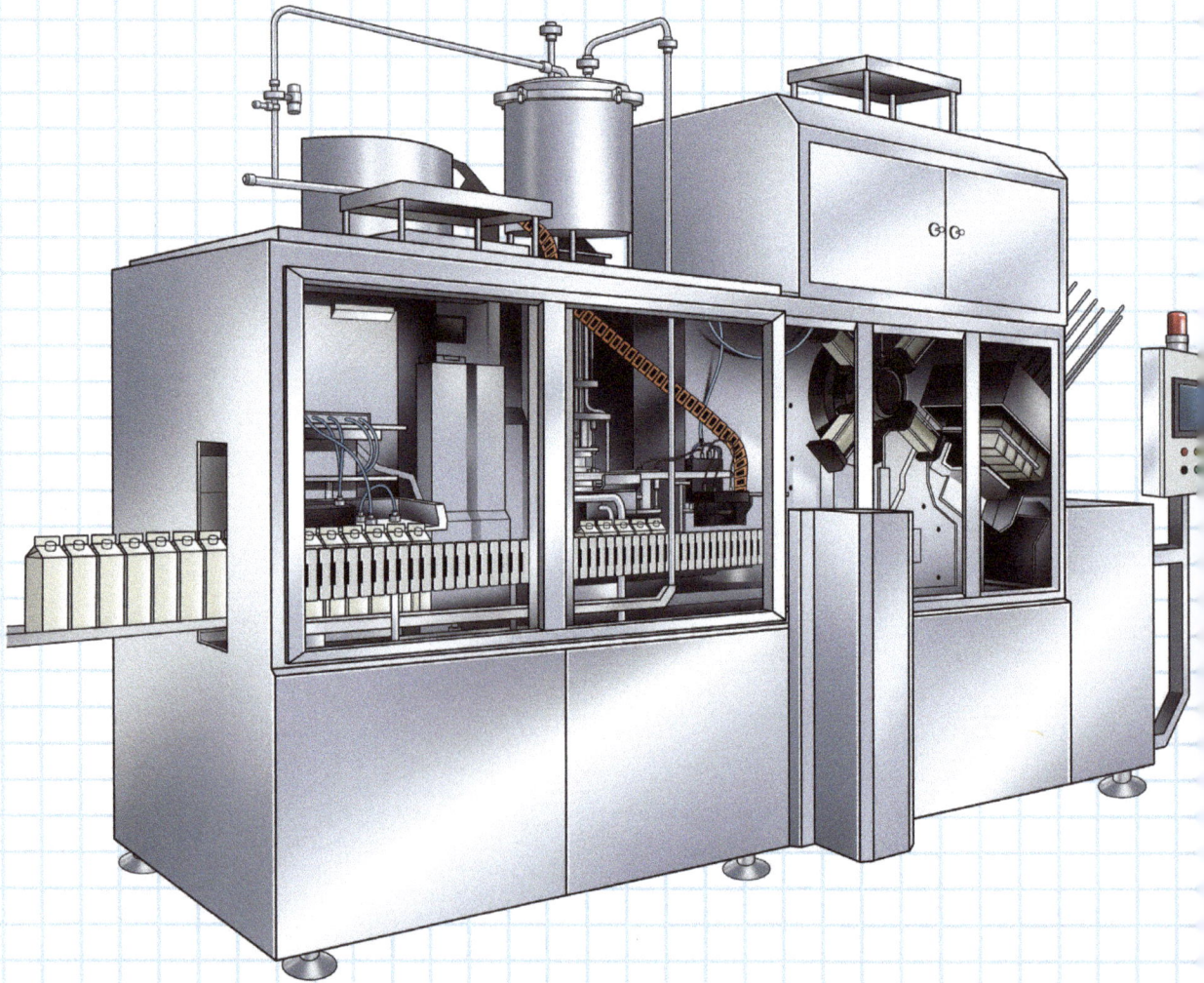

Product Packaging

The milk is gravity fed down to filling machines that package each batch into cartons and bottles of different sizes.

Crating and Distribution

Finally, the milk cartons and bottles are placed into crates for easy storage in a cold room and then onto large trucks using forklifts for distribution.

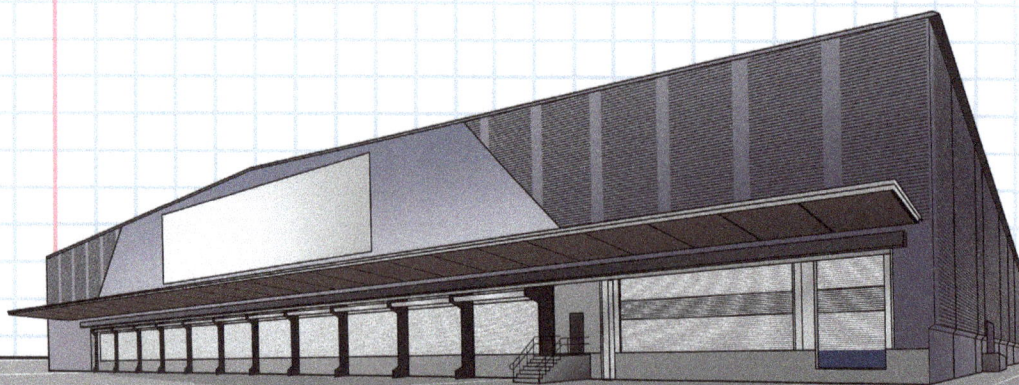

Throughout the process of preparing milk, two important **support processes** that must be performed are **Cleaning and Sanitation** and **Laboratory Testing**.

Cleaning and Sanitation

This cleaning process involves circulating water, detergent and sanitisers through the factory tanks, machinery, and process lines without dismantling equipment.

Effective and reliable cleaning and sanitation ensures the quality of the milk product is controlled.

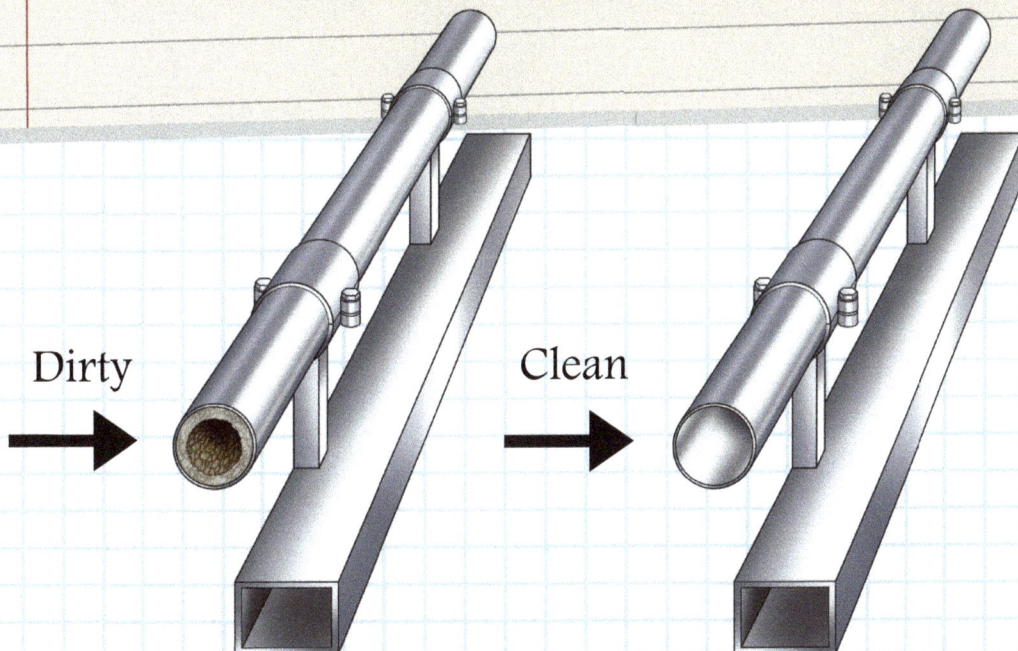

Dirty

Clean

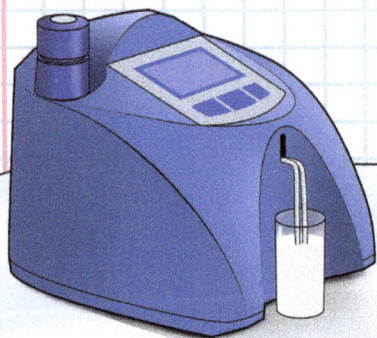
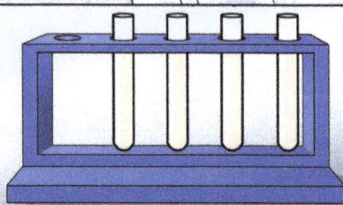
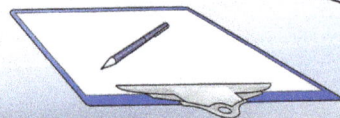

Laboratory Testing

In a laboratory, the products and raw materials are tested at all stages of production to ensure compliance to specifications and regulations.

Chemical engineers work with a cross-functional team of scientists, food technologists, even marketers who together innovate, research, and develop efficient technologies for processing milk at a commercial scale.

So, there you have it. Milk as a **liquid** ready for your morning breakfast.

But remember milk should always be stored at or below 4°C so that it reliably meets its specified use-by-date.

Chemical engineers can make a lot of things, even your favourite ice cream! But that's another story.

The End

Also By Diana Tran

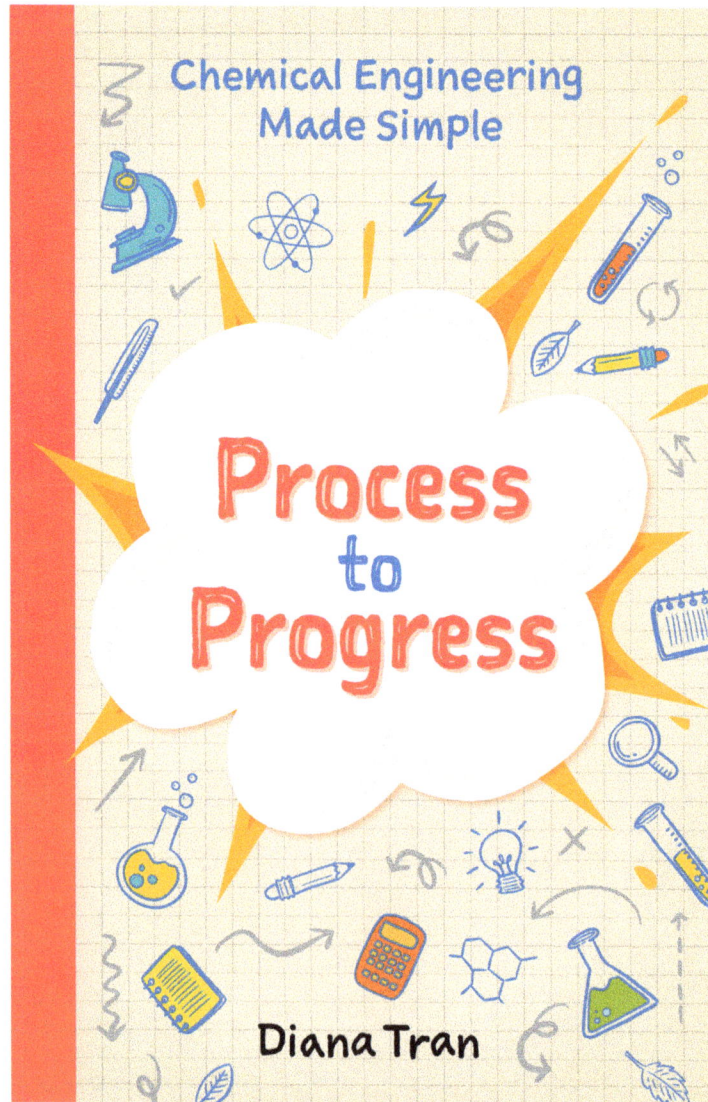

Chemical Engineering
Made Simple

Process
to
Progress

Diana Tran

www.ingramcontent.com/pod-product-compliance
Lightning Source LLC
Chambersburg PA
CBHW040250100426
42811CB00011B/1213